numicon

Geometry, Measurement and Statistics

Explorer 2

Progress Book

Name _____   Class _____

OXFORD

Date ..../ ..../ ....

Toy Trains

Can you find out how long each toy train is?

What is the difference between their lengths?

If the trains were put together, how long would they be in total?

Teacher notes

Date .... / .... / ....

How Long Is The Train?

Can you measure each train and write its length?

Lucia wants to put 3 trains together.
How long is the shortest train she can make?

How long is the longest train she can make?

How many different length trains can she make?

 Teacher notes

Date .... / .... / ....

Making Shapes

Steph has 9 geo strips.
They are all the same length.
Which polygons can she make?

Dan has 9 geo strips.
3 are short, 3 are medium, and 3 are long.
Which polygons can he make?

Can Dan make any similar shapes?

Teacher notes

Date .... / .... / ....

Kite Flying Factory

Kites are being packed in boxes at a factory.

Can you label each kite with the letters of any boxes it can go in?

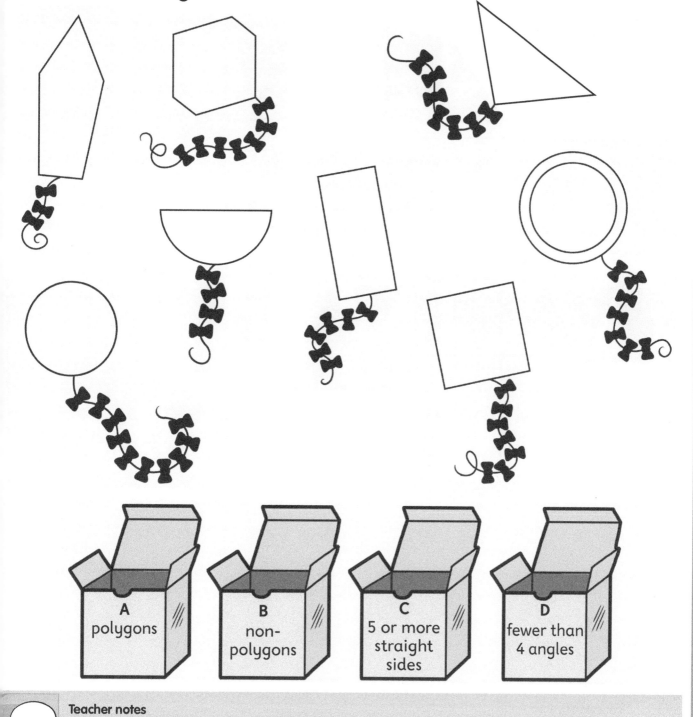

| A polygons | B non-polygons | C 5 or more straight sides | D fewer than 4 angles |

Teacher notes

Have ready:	solid geometric 3D shapes (including cubes, cuboids, pyramids, spheres, cylinders, cones, prisms), paper, paint

Date ..../ ..../ ....

Printing Patterns

Some patterns have been printed on strips of paper.

For each strip, which solid shapes could you use to copy the pattern? Use as few shapes as possible.

How many shapes are needed to make all 3 patterns? Can you use as few shapes as possible?

Teacher notes

Have ready:	solid 3D shapes or household packaging (cubes, cuboids, square-based pyramids, cylinders, cones) sticky tape or sticky labels

Date _____ / _____ / _____

Mending Toy Boxes

Some of the classroom toy boxes need mending.

Each edge and each vertex needs a piece of sticky tape. Can you work out how many pieces of sticky tape each box needs?

Toy Box	Number of Pieces of Sticky Tape	
	Edges	Vertices

Teacher notes

Have ready: 2 or 3 different colouring pencils

Date .... / .... / ....

Toy Cupboard

The toy cupboard doors need decorating.

Can you colour in oblongs to make the pattern symmetrical?

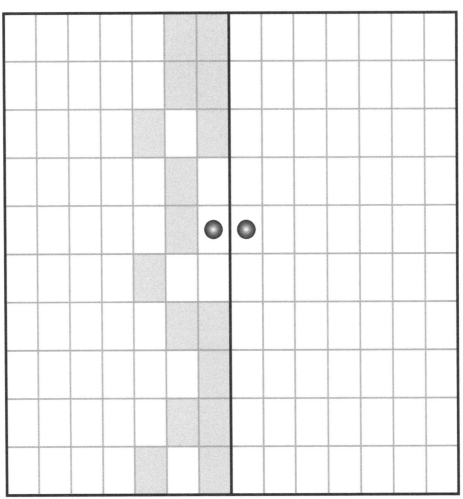

Can you use 2 or 3 different colouring pencils to add your own symmetrical pattern to the doors?

 Teacher notes

Have ready: coloured dot labels

Date .... / ..../ ....

Badge Designs

Li wants to make badges that have at least 1 line of symmetry.

Can you put a tick next to any shapes she can use?

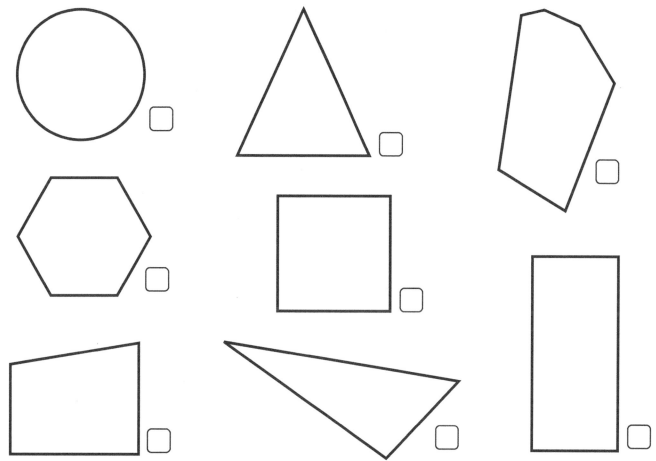

Can you use sticky coloured dots to show a symmetrical pattern on some of the badges?

You may need to draw lines of symmetry.

Teacher notes

Date .... / .... / ....

How Much?

Can you work out how much money is in each purse?

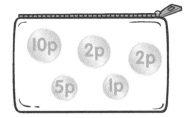

_____   _____

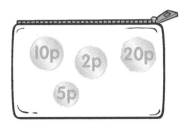

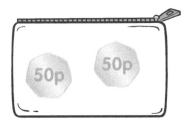

_____   _____

Choose 2 purses. Can you work out how much money is in these 2 purses in total?

Teacher notes

Date _____ / _____ / _____

George's Money Box

George has some coins in his money box. He also has some coins on the table. In total, George has exactly £1 in coins.

Can you work out how much is in the money box?

George says that he has 6 coins inside the box. What could they be?

Teacher notes

My Learning Log

My learning about shape and movement

My learning about measuring

Date .... / .... / ....

I have learned these facts.

Date .... / .... / ....

Reflections

⭐ My favourite maths was...

_____

💭 I would like more time to think about...

_____

😃 I felt proud when...

_____

Date .... / .... / ....

Seema's Savings

Seema is saving up to buy a new book that costs £8.

Can you show different ways to make £8 in the boxes below?

In 1 box, only draw coins.

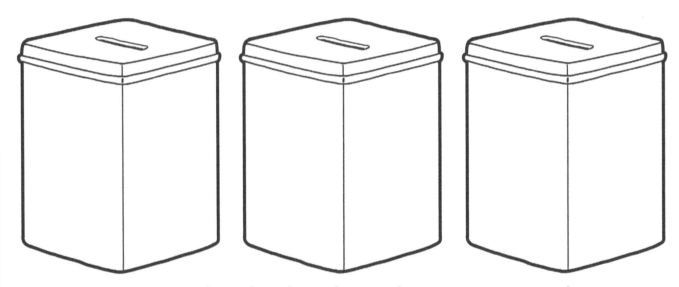

If Seema bought the book with a £10 note, how much change would she get?

Teacher notes

Date .... / .... / ....

Change From Shopping

Can you draw coins to pay for each item?
Use as few coins as possible.

 £3

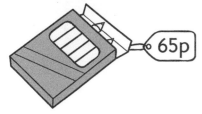 65p

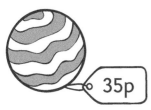 35p

If you paid for all 3 items together, which note would you use?

Can you show the change you would get?

 Teacher notes

15

Have ready: cuboids, cones, spheres, triangular prisms, cubes, squared-based pyramids, cylinders, hexagonal prisms

Date .... / .... / ....

Shape Towers

Can you use these solid shapes to build towers?

Put a cross next to any shapes that are always difficult to put at the bottom of a tower.

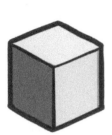   

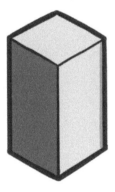   

Can you use the shapes to build towers made only from prisms?

Put a tick next to any shapes you could use.

 Teacher notes

16

Have ready: 3D solid prisms and/or 'real-life' boxes to use as models for the soaps or small soaps (cuboids, triangular prisms, hexagonal prisms)

Date .... / .... / ....

Soap Boxes

3 bars of soap stack together in a box.

Can you work out how many faces each box has?

How might the boxes change if 3 more bars are put on top of each stack?

Do you think anything about the boxes would stay the same?

Teacher notes

Date .... / .... / ....

Adventure Park

8 children are visiting an adventure park.

Their teacher wants to know how many tickets to buy for each ride.

The children want to know if there will be enough of them on each ride for them to sit in pairs.

Can you use the information to complete the table? Choose a ride for each child to go on.

A
1 m or shorter

B
95 cm to 1 m 25 cm

C
1 m 20 cm or taller

Artem 90 cm	Sophia 1 m 30 cm
Ed 84 cm	Peter 1 m 23 cm
Tom 1 m 10 cm	Lakisha 1 m 3 cm
Jess 96 cm	Agata 1 m 25 cm

	Height	Ride A, B or C?
Artem	90 cm	A
Sophia		
Ed		
Peter		
Tom		
Lakisha		
Jess		
Agata		

Teacher notes

Date .... / .... / ....

Adventure Park

Can you use the information from your table to complete this block graph?

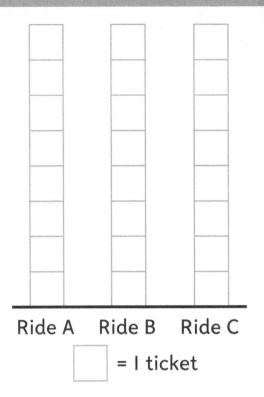

Ride A   Ride B   Ride C

= 1 ticket

How many tickets should the teacher buy for each ride?

Can the children sit in pairs on each ride?

Which ride has the most children?

Teacher notes

Date .... / .... / ....

Balancing Act

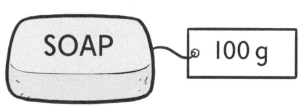

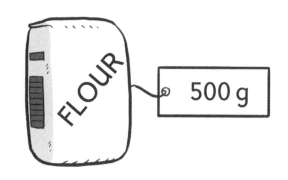

Can you draw bars of soap or bags of flour in the pan balances to make them balance?

Can you draw a different combination in each empty pan?

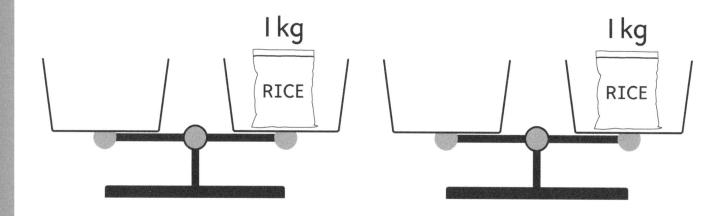

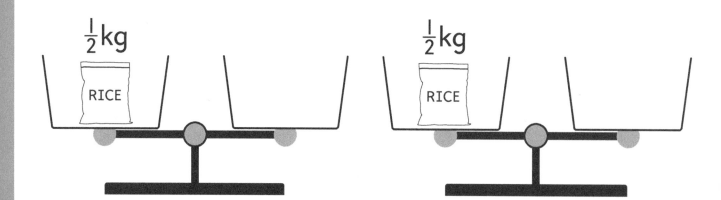

Teacher notes

Date ..../ ..../ ....

Shopping

There are lots of each of these items in the shop.

$\frac{1}{4}$ kg $\frac{1}{2}$ kg   I kg

Sam can carry I$\frac{1}{2}$ kg of food home from the shop.

Can you show what different combinations of food he can buy?

Teacher notes

Date .... / .... / ....

Measuring Water

Can you work out how much water is in each of these jugs?

Each jug needs to have a litre of water in it.

How much more water needs to be added to each jug?

 Teacher notes

22

Date _____ / _____ / _____

Holiday Temperatures

Jenny is on holiday. She checks the temperature at midday.

Can you write what the temperature was on Saturday and Sunday?

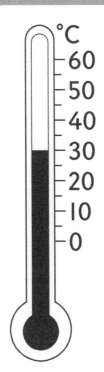

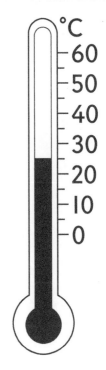

Saturday _____   Sunday _____

What might the temperature be at midnight?

Can you fill in the thermometers and write the temperatures?

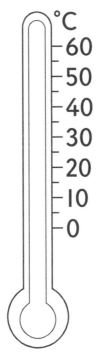

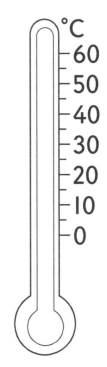

Saturday
midnight _____

Saturday
midnight _____

Teacher notes

Date _____ / _____ / _____

Telling The Time

Can you draw the hour and minute hands on the clocks to show the times of each event today?

Can you write the time under each clock?

School starts

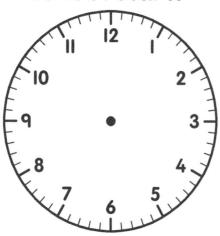

_____

Lunch time starts

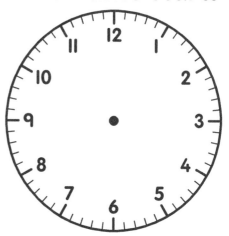

_____

School finishes

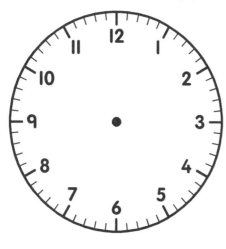

_____

Bed time

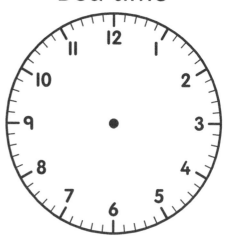

_____

 Teacher notes

Date ..../ ..../ ....

Train Ride

Amy and her mum get the 9 o'clock train to the beach.

The journey takes 3 hours.

Can you show what time they get there?

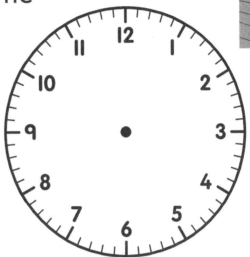

The journey home takes 4 hours.

They get home at 25 minutes past 8.

Can you show what time they left the beach?

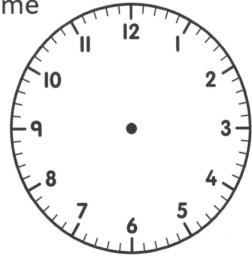

 Teacher notes

25

Have ready: Numicon Shapes, colouring pencils

Date .... / .... / ....

Turning Shapes

Can you continue this rotating shape pattern?

Can you colour in squares to make your own rotating shape pattern?

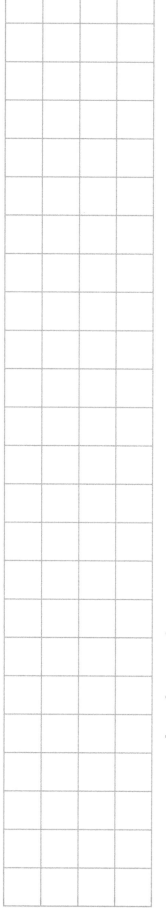

Teacher notes

Date .... / .... / ....

Have ready: small shapes or objects for children to draw round onto their sails

Paper Windmills

Choose a shape.

Can you draw around it on 1 of the sails on this windmill?

Imagine the windmill rotating.

Can you draw around the same shape on every sail to make a rotating pattern?

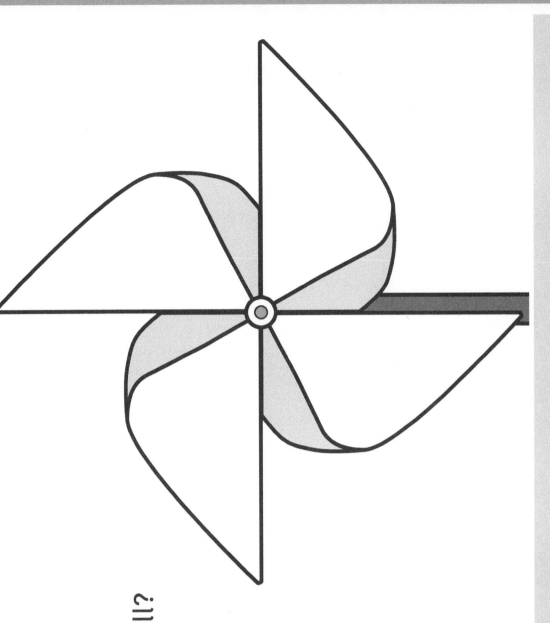

Teacher notes

My Learning Log

My learning about shape and movement

My learning about measuring

I have learned these facts.

Reflections

⭐ <u>My favourite maths was…</u>

💭 <u>I would like more time to think about…</u>

😊 <u>I felt proud when…</u>

Date .... / .... / ....

Pocket Money

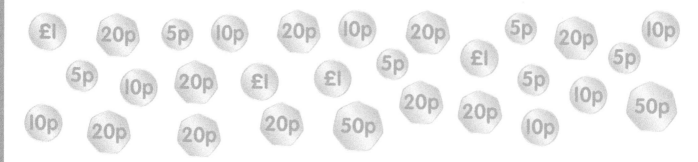

Can you use tally marks to help Becky find out how many of each coin she has?

Coin	Tally	Number of Coins	Value
5p			
10p			
20p			
50p			
£1			

Becky wants to buy a toy that costs £10. Does she have enough money?

Can you draw coins to show the difference between Becky's money and the cost of the toy?

Teacher notes

Have ready: colouring pencils

Date .... / .... / ....

Brothers And Sisters

Ask each child in your class how many brothers and sisters they have. Fill in this table to tally your results.

Number of Brothers and Sisters	Tally	Total
0		
1		
2		
3		
4 or more		

Can you use your totals to draw a block graph?

Choose a number for each block to represent.

 =

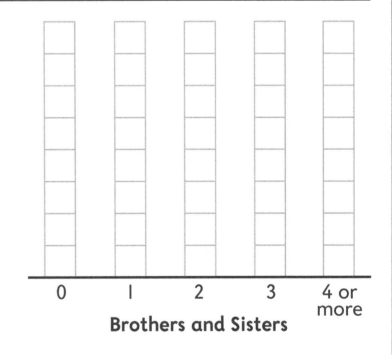

Brothers and Sisters

What do you notice?

 Teacher notes

numicon

Geometry, Measurement and Statistics

Explorer 2
Progress Book

Can you show a symmetrical pattern on the turtle?

Your **Explorer Progress book 2** contains:

- Fun activities that give you a chance to show what you understand and what you are thinking.

- Learning Logs where you can record what you know and what you can do.

  ⭐ Say what your favourite piece of work was.

  💬 Say what you need more time to think about.

  😊 Say what you were most proud of.

Information for your teacher

The activities in this book match the activity groups in the Teaching Resource Handbook for Geometry, Measurement and Statistics 2. In the top right-hand corner of each page, you can see which activity group it matches.

A range of apparatus should be freely available to children as they work on the activities. The 'Have ready' box at the top of the page shows specific resource requirements where appropriate.

Use the 'Teacher notes' section of each page to give children feedback.

OXFORD
UNIVERSITY PRESS

Great Clarendon Street, Oxford, OX2 6DP,
United Kingdom

Oxford University Press is a department of the University of Oxford. It furthers the University's objective of excellence in research, scholarship, and education by publishing worldwide.
Oxford is a registered trade mark of Oxford University Press in the UK and in certain other countries

Text and illustrations © Oxford University Press 2014
Typeset by Tech-Set Ltd, Gateshead
Figurative artworks by JHS Studio
Cover artwork by David Semple
Written by Simon d'Angelo, Elizabeth Gibbs, Andrew Jeffrey, Sue Lowndes and Dr Tony Wing
The moral rights of the authors have been asserted.

This edition published 2014

ISBN 978-0-19-838953-8

10 9 8 7 6 5

Printed in Great Britain by Ashford Colour Press

Oxford OWL

For teachers
Helping you with free eBooks, inspirational resources, advice and support

For parents
Helping your child's learning with free eBooks, essential tips and fun activities

www.oxfordowl.co.uk

OXFORD
UNIVERSITY PRESS

How to get in touch:
web www.oxfordprimary.co.uk
email schools.enquiries.uk@oup.com
tel. +44 (0) 1536 452610
fax +44 (0) 1865 313472

ISBN 978-0-19-838953-8

9 780198 389538